13905557R00060

Printed in Great Britain
by Amazon